302.302
LEA

DATE DUE

Pattonville High School Library
2497 Creve Coeur Mill Road
Maryland Heights, MO 63043

COMBATTING SHAMING and Toxic Communities™

COMBATTING TOXIC ONLINE COMMUNITIES

AMIE JANE LEAVITT

Pattonville High School Library
2497 Creve Coeur Road
Maryland Heights, MO 63043

Published in 2017 by The Rosen Publishing Group, Inc.
29 East 21st Street, New York, NY 10010

Copyright © 2017 by The Rosen Publishing Group, Inc.

First Edition

All rights reserved. No part of this book may be reproduced in any form without permission in writing from the publisher, except by a reviewer.

Library of Congress Cataloging-in-Publication Data

Names: Leavitt, Amie Jane, author.
Title: Combatting toxic online communities / Amie Jane Leavitt.
Description: New York : Rosen Publishing, 2017. | Series: Combatting shaming and toxic communities | Audience: Grades 7-12. | Includes bibliographical references and index.
Identifiers: LCCN 2015050278 | ISBN 9781508171171 (library bound)
Subjects: LCSH: Online social networks--Juvenile literature. | Online hate speech--Juvenile literature.
Classification: LCC HM742 .L385 2016 | DDC 302.30285--dc23
LC record available at http://lccn.loc.gov/2015050278

Manufactured in China

CONTENTS

4 INTRODUCTION

7 CHAPTER 1
JUMPING ON THE BANDWAGON

18 CHAPTER 2
WHERE NOBODY KNOWS YOUR NAME

30 CHAPTER 3
HOW WILL YOU RESPOND?

41 CHAPTER 4
A BRIGHT ONLINE FUTURE

50 GLOSSARY
52 FOR MORE INFORMATION
57 FOR FURTHER READING
59 BIBLIOGRAPHY
62 INDEX

INTRODUCTION

An online community is a group of people who share a common interest and meet and communicate with each other on the Internet. Some communities are positive. Members of cancer support groups, for example, include patients and their family members who are in all stages of the disease. Members of the group can pose questions and concerns, and other members will offer their advice and support based on their own experiences. There are many online communities focused on positive topics, including blogs, forums, and social media pages that try to enhance and uplift the lives of all of their members. Some are based on health and fitness. Some are focused on home improvements and other DIY projects. Some are dedicated to hobbies such as cooking, knitting, camping, and gardening.

However, there are also many communities on the Internet that have a very toxic reputation. Their goal is to spew hatred, prejudice, and violence online. These groups use the argument that speech should be free, especially online speech, and that they should be able to say whatever they want to whomever they want whenever they want.

But is freedom of speech really free? Can you really say whatever you want without any consequences? In the real world, the answer is definitely no. If you make a threat toward someone, for example, you can find yourself in serious legal trouble. But so

INTRODUCTION

Websites can have Terms of Service (TOS) that denote the type of behavior that is expected of members. When properly enforced, TOS help limit toxicity in online communities.

far, the online world has been different. Some communities have clear rules and enforce them. Other communities have no rules. They allow freedom of speech no matter what. The fact that few people actually use their real-life identities online also spurs the lack of accountability for what is said online, too.

Among the various negative online communities out there, according to the Southern Poverty Law Center, Reddit has a reputation of being one of the most toxic. Reddit is an online bulletin board that prides itself on allowing its members unfettered freedom of speech. On Reddit, members can form their own subreddits, or communities, which can be on any topic. Some are positive and relatively harmless and offer opportunities for their members to engage in lively conversation. Other communities are founded on topics that are extremely harmful, hurtful, and dangerous—they promote racism, violence against women, prejudices against religious and minority groups, and hatred toward really anyone for anything. No one is exempt from the toxic rhetoric found on the negative subreddits. As of 2015, changes have been made to Reddit's user policy to help mitigate some of this toxicity, but a lot of the negativity remains. After all, it's very difficult to monitor a site that has more than 160 million users around the world.

Certainly, Reddit isn't alone in its toxicity. The comments sections of websites are synonymous with negativity as well. According to the *New York Times*, trolls, people who "post inflammatory, derogatory, or provocative messages in public forums," will often try to stir up trouble online and get other people on board with their negativity. Cyberbullies, individuals who use the Internet to harass or intentionally harm others, are found in all kinds of online communities: forums, message boards, Twitter, Facebook, online gaming, personal blogs, chat rooms, and so forth.

What causes some sites to be positive and others to be so negative? And is there anything that can be done to combat the toxicity of online communities?

These questions will be explored in greater depth throughout the course of this resource as we dig deep into the roots of online toxicity and offer some possible suggestions for solutions.

JUMPING ON THE BANDWAGON

Online communities experience many of the same problems that real communities experience. It's human nature for people to want to fit in. Sometimes, people will even sacrifice their own individuality in order to do so. They'll go along with whatever the group is doing, just so they can appear to be part of the group. The term "jumping on the bandwagon" is a common phrase used to describe this typical human behavior. If you've ever wondered where this phrase comes from, imagine the following:

> A group of people are lining an old-time parade route, and the circus-type wagon at the beginning of the parade holds a festive musical group playing a toe-tapping tune. There's something so mesmerizing about the music that people are drawn toward it. Some of the spectators leave their positions along the parade route, run alongside the "bandwagon," and jump on to join the musicians. Others see how

fun this looks and do the same. After all, they don't want to be left out. Soon, the wagon is overflowing—there are more people inside the bandwagon than there are on the sidelines.

You would never put on a blindfold and follow someone off a cliff. However, this can happen very easily in a symbolic sense if we don't think and act for ourselves, both offline and online.

The description of this scene helps show one of the saying's literal meanings, and it also gives clues to the phrase's symbolic meaning, too. When people say, "jumping on the bandwagon," they are referring to the desire that people feel when they support something only because it appears to be the popular thing to do. Everyone's doing it, so why not me? I want to fit in, too!

Jumping on a bandwagon can be a good thing if the cause is good. When groups of people work together to accomplish a service project, community event, or other act of goodwill, they can achieve great results. But what if the cause isn't a good one? What then? When groups of people jump on a negative bandwagon together, the results can be quite destructive. This type of behavior isn't new to the Internet, and it's not new to our twenty-first-century society either. Rather, there are many examples of situations like this that have happened throughout history. One of the most famous ones occurred in seventeeth-century New England in a little town called Salem, Massachusetts.

The Salem Witch Trials

In the spring of 1692, a group of young girls in Salem village claimed to be possessed by the devil. In order to explain their fits and delirium, they immediately accused several women in the community of witchcraft. These initial accusations set off a firestorm of other accusations until nearly every family in the community was affected by the "witch hunt" in some way. During the Salem Witch Trials, more than two hundred people in the community were accused of practicing witchcraft—a crime that was punishable by death.

No one was exempt from these accusations. The old and infirm were lifted from their sick beds and brought to trial.

Prominent members of the community were indicted. Even children as young as four years old were implicated. Ironically, the group could have stood together and demanded that the madness stop. However, that is not what happened. In fact, it was the group together as a cohesive whole that allowed the accusations and witch hunt to continue.

Most of this behavior was based on fear. Speaking out in an accused person's defense could mean that you were a witch, too. So, because of that, many people kept quiet. They distanced themselves from the accused in a form of self-preservation. They lurked in the shadows hoping they wouldn't be noticed and

The Salem Witch Trials are a reminder of the dangers of groupthink. However, the lessons learned from these tragic events can help people make better decisions today.

accused next. Some people did speak out, of course. But they did so at their own peril.

Not only was the fear based on self-preservation, but also on suspicion. What if all of these people really were witches? They certainly couldn't be left to contaminate the rest of the community. If everyone else agreed that these people were witches—if the judges and witness all said they were—then maybe they were! It was this type of mentality that also led the community as a whole to support the accusations and convictions of the innocent that were taking place in their little village.

The accused had one easy way out. If they were to admit to their crime, promise repentance, and name the person who had "bewitched" them, they would be exonerated. However, that method of acquittal just perpetuated the finger-pointing and accusations and left anyone a target.

Some people used this lifesaving strategy. Others refused. Their reasons were generally twofold. For one, because of their strong Puritan upbringing, they couldn't admit to doing something that they had not done, especially something as heinous as aligning with the devil. For another, they had too much integrity to point the finger of blame at someone else just to save their own lives. Because of that, these individuals were convicted and sentenced to death. Nineteen in total were hung at Gallows Hill, and one man was crushed to death under a pile of boulders.

Explanations from Human Psychology

The horrific events that occurred in this small Puritan community more than three hundred years ago are definitely a blight on American history. However, the human psychology that caused the Salem Witch Trials and other events like it throughout history unfortunately still continues to cause tragic events in contemporary communities today, and even in online communities.

Psychologists have labeled this type of behavior mob mentality. Mob mentality occurs in groups when individuals lose their sense of self-awareness and behave differently than they would if they were all alone. In mob mentality, individuals follow the crowd, jump on the bandwagon, and will sometimes exhibit inappropriate, dangerous, or violent behaviors. They get caught up in what everyone else is doing and follow suit. Often, individuals don't even think about any possible personal consequences of

The "everyone's doing it!" mentality can lead to extreme behavior that individuals wouldn't necessarily exhibit outside of the group atmosphere. Think about a sale that excites shoppers so much that they are willing to push and shove others.

their behavior—in their mind they believe they certainly can't be held responsible since the entire "group" did it and not just them. This lack of accountability thereby encourages more of the negative behavior to occur. Also, the larger the group, the more people lose their self-awareness and become willing to engage in more inappropriate or even dangerous behavior.

Don Forsyth, a professor at the University of Richmond and expert on group dynamics, was interviewed by Lacy Schley in May 2012 regarding mob mentalities. In the article, titled "Mob Mentality Can Take Over Protests or Even Clearance Sales," for the Northwestern University Medill Reports, Forsyth explains, "Conformity increases in mobs, as people do what everyone else is doing. So, if the mob develops unusual 'situational norms,' then the majority of the group members will do that—resulting in what looks like mob mentality. In most cases, the strong mob actions occur when people are part of a group with which they identify."

The events that happened in the Salem Witch Trials continue to happen to some degree today. In the online world, "witch hunts" can occur often, especially in toxic communities. Many communities forbid their users from posting other people's personal information on their sites in an effort to ban online witch hunts from turning into real-life ones. However, unfortunately, that doesn't stop people from using online communities and social media to try to destroy another person's life.

There are many examples of Internet mob mentalities that have caused damage to individuals and organizations. One example of a mob mentality and witch hunt occurred in the summer of 2015.

FALSELY ACCUSED

In April 2013, a twenty-two-year-old college student named Sunil Tripathi was falsely accused by a Reddit member of being a suspect in the 2013 Boston Marathon bombings. The Internet latched on to the Reddit "lead" and started an online witch hunt. The national media joined the bandwagon, too. Tripathi had been missing for over a month and his family had been desperately trying to find him. They set up a Facebook page to let him know that they loved him and wanted him to come home. People began posting horrible messages on the page regarding Tripathi's suspected involvement in the bombings. The family eventually took down the Facebook page because they couldn't bear to read any more of the horrible messages. The FBI continued its investigation and found the suspects. Tripathi was not one of them. Reddit issued the Tripathi family its apologies for the witch hunt that began on Reddit. However, the damage had already been done. Tripathi's already traumatized family became even more traumatized by the way their missing son had been treated by the online world.

So, how should a situation like this have been handled? If a person thinks he or she recognizes an individual that authorities are looking for, that person should not get online and make a bunch of wild accusations about who the individual might be. If a person has a credible lead and thinks he or she recognizes a suspect, that person should call the authorities and report it. Then, that person should let the authorities investigate. If everyone were to do this, online witch hunts and vigilante justice would be thwarted. There is absolutely no place for either of those methods in a lawful society. If people leave the investigation to the authorities and do not become "armchair detectives," the innocent can remain innocent until proved guilty by a court of law.

The Cecil the Lion Witch Hunt

It was in July 2015 that the Internet world became outraged when news broke of the death of Cecil, a beloved lion on a protected wildlife preserve in Africa. Brent Stapelkamp, a field researcher who had been studying Cecil since 2008, told *National Geographic*, "Cecil was the ultimate lion. He was everything that a lion represents to us as humans. He was large, powerful, but regal at the same time." Tourists and scientists loved this special lion, who was known for his gentleness, beauty, and for his unusual long, black mane.

The story of Cecil's death was a complicated one. The facts trickled in slowly, and conflicting accounts arose. Cecil was shot by a big game hunter, a dentist from the United States named Walter Palmer. The details were a little sketchy as to the events that unfolded during the hunt. Reports claimed that the lion was lured out of the reserve. Palmer claimed that he didn't know he was hunting a protected lion and that he had hired professional guides who he counted on to take him on a legal hunt.

COMBATTING TOXIC ONLINE COMMUNITIES

Cecil the lion, the beloved feline known for his black-tinged mane, was killed in a trophy hunt in July 2015. His hunter, a US dentist, became the target of a viral hate campaign, complete with death threats.

It didn't matter what the specifics of the event were. Mass hysteria still broke out. It didn't take long at all for subreddits, blogs, and the social media world to go wild with its limited information and demand vigilante justice. People went out of their minds in a worldwide showcase of mob mentality. Palmer quickly became one of the most hated men in the world. His name, address, and place of business were posted all over the Internet. People shouted out all kinds of obscenities and bombarded his dental website with vitriol. Within days, Palmer had to close down his dental practice and go into hiding with his family because of the mountain of death threats that came pouring in. The witch hunt had begun.

People seemed to feed off of each other, as they generally do in a mob mentality. Each online post brought a thunderstorm of others. Individuals tried to outdo each other with the hate-filled speech that they spewed at Palmer.

So, here is the question: Was Palmer right in his actions in killing Cecil the lion? The answer to that question is simply not something that the public has any right to decide. That is not how law and order in a lawful society works. The question of his innocence or guilt is supposed to be decided by a court of law, not by the general public using vigilante justice.

Regardless of the correctness of Palmer's actions, what most absolutely is not right is the way the public responded. Destroying a person and his reputation through an online mob mentality is not right in any situation. And what is absolutely and definitively not right is to make threats against someone's life. It doesn't matter if you mean them or not—you don't make those kinds of threats. Period. It is not morally right, and it is definitely not legal to do so. It does not matter what the person has done or what the public thinks that person has done, there is absolutely no excuse for this type of behavior.

Walter Palmer's treatment became 2015's prime example of the dangers that can occur when a mob mentality takes over the online world. There was no escape for this man. Essentially, everyone everywhere had the ability to throw their stones and sling their arrows of hatred at Palmer, and he was powerless to make it stop.

So, here's a question to ponder: If this can happen to Walter Palmer for what he did, then could it realistically happen to anyone else for actions that the public collectively deems inappropriate, whether or not the public is correct? Could it happen to innocent people whose actions the public perceives as wrong? The answer is yes, and it already has.

WHERE NOBODY KNOWS YOUR NAME

The 1980's television show *Cheers* became famous for its tagline "Where everybody knows your name." The idea was that people on the show loved to come to *Cheers* because it was a place where everyone knew each other, there was a sense of community, and people felt like they were all friends.

While the Internet can also be a place where people feel a sense of community, the connections made online are virtual and generally done in an anonymous way. So it could be said that the online world, unlike the real world, is actually a place where *nobody* knows your name. Often people avoid using their real names in their Internet handles—they instead find some clever or cute name to go by that often has no connection to who they really are. That gives them a cloak of anonymity.

The Internet naturally provides an environment where people can be anonymous. In 1993, the *New Yorker* published a cartoon by Peter Steiner. It shows a dog sitting at a computer desk with his hand on the keyboard. He is speaking to another dog that is sitting on the floor next to him. The dog's words are shown in the caption, which reads, "On the Internet, nobody knows you're a dog." The Internet was in its infancy when this cartoon was published—yet the overall atmosphere of the Internet is still

WHERE NOBODY KNOWS YOUR NAME

Who is the person behind that Internet handle? The cloak of anonymity that the Internet provides can cause some people to behave in ways they normally wouldn't.

the same. Essentially, anyone can be anonymous online if they decide to make it that way.

This sense of anonymity is another reason (besides the mob mentality) that online communities can become toxic environments. When people hide behind a mask or cloak of anonymity, they often find it easy to behave differently than they would in real life simply because they know they can get away with it. Under this mask, they may start to believe that if no one *really* knows who they are, then it doesn't matter how they act, what they say, what they do, or how they treat others.

Analyzing the Online World

Psychologists are naturally interested in the behavior of the online world. In fact, an entire new branch of psychology has emerged because of the Internet. It is called cyberpsychology, and it involves the study of how people behave individually and in groups online. John Suler, a professor of psychology at Rider University, has written extensively on research in cyberpsychology. His article "The Online Disinhibition Effect" explores in depth

In the real world, heated debates can lead to physical confrontations. People feel less inhibited online because those physical consequences don't appear to exist. People can lash out and then slip away into the shadows.

the behavior of Internet users. He explains that the "disinhibition effect" allows people to feel less inhibited or restricted online. When the disinhibition effect becomes toxic, people engage in "rude language, harsh criticisms, anger, hatred, and even threats." Essentially, people who are generally polite and well-mannered in real life can behave in very inappropriate ways online.

There are many causes of the disinhibition effect. One is anonymity. Suler explains that when people aren't linked to their real-life identities, "they don't have to own their behavior by acknowledging it within the full context of who they 'really' are. When acting out hostile feelings, the person doesn't have to take responsibility for those actions. In fact, people might even convince themselves that those behaviors 'aren't me at all.'"

Another reason that people feel less inhibited online is the idea of invisibility. Even if someone actually knows the people in his or her online community in real life, there seems to be less shyness about what is said online. Suler explains that when you communicate online, others can't see you or your expressions and you can't see theirs. "Seeing a frown, a shaking head, a sigh, a bored expression, and many other subtle and not so subtle signs of disapproval or indifference can slam the breaks on what people are willing to express," Suler explains.

Gamers Behaving Badly

The online gaming community is known for its negativity. Wil Wheaton wrote about this topic in his article for the *Washington Post* titled "Anonymous Trolls Are Destroying Online Games. Here's How to Stop Them." He explained that because gamers rarely have to see the people they play against, this encourages them to behave badly.

COMBATTING TOXIC ONLINE COMMUNITIES

> Online gaming can be a fun way to connect with people from around the world. However, it can also be a place where behavior is at its most reckless and toxic.

Back when Wheaton first started playing video games, he had to go to an arcade to play. "We had to win and lose with grace, or we'd get our butts beaten (literally) by other players." Later, when video games moved into living rooms, players sat next to each other while they played. Yes, they could "talk and razz each other," Wheaton explains, but they did so with respect. "Playing games with real, live humans prevented any of the poisonous behavior proliferating online today." Wheaton feels strongly that gamers need to stop acting so negatively online. "It's time to break this cycle—and to teach gamers that they . . . can win and lose without spewing racist, misogynist, homophobic bile at their fellow gamers. But doing so requires casting off the cloak of anonymity."

Shocking Mommies

Online communities of all sorts experience issues with anonymity and poor behavior. One would assume the mommy blogosphere would be a very positive place where mothers support each other with their various parenting dilemmas. While that is true in some instances, in others, mommy bloggers are frequent victims of trolls and harassment in the comments sections of their articles. Rebecca Eckler is one of those bloggers who has experienced the negative effects of trolls. The articles on her mommy blog can be quite controversial. However, instead of people just refusing

Mommies can be haters, too. The mommy blogger scene has seen its fair share of judgement, negativity, and toxicity over the years.

to read her articles if they don't agree with them, they instead post horrible, mean-spirited, vitriolic remarks in the comments section of her website. These aren't isolated events either. They went on for years when she was running her blog. Eckler wrote a book about her experience titled *The Mommy Mob*.

Annie of the *PhD In Parenting* blog wrote about Eckler's book and the negative comments that are prevalent in the mommy blogosphere in her article "The Nasty Trolls of the Mommy Mob." She said, "There is paparazzi style stalking of some bloggers, there are people who have Child Protective Services sent to bloggers' homes, and there are people who have called bloggers' employers. I'm not immune to the appeal of a little gossip here and there (no one is perfect), but some of this stuff is unbelievable, pathetic and even dangerous." So, even in the world of mommies and children, toxicity can reign online.

Taking Personal Responsibility

While mob mentality and anonymity are clearly two of the reasons that toxicity exists in online communities, they certainly aren't the only ones. Experts also agree that a general lack of civility and personal accountability are also to blame. Katherine Cross, a sociologist at the City University of New York, was quoted in a *Wired* magazine article titled "Why Outlawing Anonymity Will Not Halt Online Abuse" by Katie Collins. In this article, Cross explains her views on online accountability: "People say awful things to each other and to large groups of people on Facebook because they know they can get away with it. They understand that there is no accountability for bad behavior on the Internet."

Cross's point is very valid. On Facebook, people generally show their own identity and they know the people they correspond with. So, while anonymity is a problem in some situations, a larger problem is the accountability issue. After all, if people held themselves personally responsible for their own actions, then whether they were speaking anonymously or not, they would exhibit proper behavior. The hard truth of that is, however, that some people will do that and some people will not. For those who will not behave properly online out of intrinsic reasons, they need to know that there will be some kind of retribution for bad behavior. Just as when a person does something inappropriate in real life they will experience specific consequences, there need to be consequences in the online world, too.

ARE YOU BEHAVING APPROPRIATELY ONLINE?

It's easy to point the finger at others and look at ways that they can improve their online behavior. But what about you? Do you behave appropriately online, or are there ways that you can become a better online citizen and leave a positive digital footprint. After all, personal accountability is the number one way to improve everyone's experiences online. Take this quiz. Then think about your answers. Perhaps there's at least one way that you can find to improve your online behavior.

(continued on the next page)

COMBATTING TOXIC ONLINE COMMUNITIES

(continued from previous page)

1. Do you obey the law online? On an even higher level, do you obey a basic code of conduct and behave ethically?

2. Do you live by the golden rule? Meaning: Do you treat others online like you would want to be treated?

3. Take that to another level. Do you treat others the way they would want to be treated? Do you think about others' feelings before you say something, post a picture, or post a video about them?

4. Are you doing things just because "everybody else is doing it," even if it's not right?

5. Would you be willing to act this way and say these things in your *real life*?

6. Would you act this way in front of your friends, your family, your parents, your teachers, your school administrators, or a police officer?

7. Would you behave this way if your real name was used?

8. Are you acting in a certain way just because you feel strong emotions about it (annoyed, angry, envious, etc.)? Or are you taking the time to cool off before you post something online?

9. Are you making sure you communicate your ideas and thoughts clearly, knowing that the written word cannot indicate sarcasm and tone of voice?

10. How do you feel about yourself and the way you behave online? Do you feel proud or do you feel ashamed?

Getting a Grip

Many online communities have tried to get a better handle on the behavior on their sites. Reddit, for example, instituted a new policy in March 2015 that clarified its harassment policy. It says:

Do not threaten, harass, or bully
> We do not tolerate the harassment of people on our site, nor do we tolerate communities dedicated to fostering harassing behavior.
>
> Harassment on Reddit is defined as systematic and/or continued actions to torment or demean someone in a way that would make a reasonable person conclude that Reddit is not a safe platform to express their ideas or participate in the conversation, or fear for their safety or the safety of those around them.
>
> Being annoying, vote brigading, or participating in a heated argument is not harassment, but following an individual or group of users, online or off, to the point where they no longer feel that it's safe to post online or are in fear of their real life safety is.

The gamer communities have also implemented ways to curb online harassment. Microsoft's Xbox Network relies on its reputation system to thwart players from behaving badly. Each user is given a color-coded rating, which is determined by a computerized system based on player feedback. Green = Good Player; Yellow = Questionable Behavior; Red = Avoid Me!

COMBATTING TOXIC ONLINE COMMUNITIES

Some video games have instituted tribunals, similar to juries. Peer enforcement of online rules has proved to be quite successful for some online communities.

League of Legends, which is the one of the most popular video games in the world, has a very interesting way of curbing inappropriate behavior among its gamers. It has set up a tribunal—which is a jury of fellow players who vote on the punishment for bad behavior reported by users. The punishment can simply be an e-mail warning to the misbehaving gamer. Or it can be a long-term ban. Not only are players with poor behavior punished, players with good behavior are rewarded. According to its website, it wants to "reward players who exemplify the best sportsmanship in *League of Legends.*"

An article in *Wired* magazine titled "Curbing Online Abuse Isn't Impossible. Here's Where We Start" by Edel Rodriguez explained a very interesting result of the *League of Legends* tribunal system. "This system is not just punishing players; it's rehabilitating them, elevating more than 280,000 censured gamers to good standing," Rodriguez explains. Apparently, those members who go through the tribunal system regularly apologize, saying "they hadn't understood how offensive their behavior was until it was pointed out to them."

Essentially, when people know there are specific standards that need to be met and are held accountable for those standards, behavior generally improves. Rodriguez's idea of how to curb negative behavior is by making sure the guidelines on websites and the enforcement of those guidelines mimic real-life communities. His recommendations are to "involve users in the moderation process, set defaults that create hurdles to abuse, give clearer feedback for people who misbehave, and—above all—create a norm in which harassment simply isn't tolerated."

It's refreshing to know that online communities are trying to take action and help create more positive environments on their sites. Hopefully, even more communities will follow suit and come up with ways to promote constructive dialogue and entertaining experiences in an environment that respects all of its members.

HOW WILL YOU RESPOND?

Sometimes, you don't know how you'll respond to a situation until you're actually in the situation. However, instead of being blindsided and forced to make decisions on the fly, it's better to look at scenarios and come up with a game plan of how you'd like to respond. So, let's look at three possible online experiences and examine ways that would be best to deal with them.

Scenario #1

You are playing an online game with other gamers around the globe. During the game, a few of the other players start to speak with very obscene language. In their descriptions, they use racial slurs, denigrate minority groups, and use hateful speech toward women. Then, they start lashing out at one of the other players in the group and start directing their hate-filled speech toward this individual. What should you do?

HOW WILL YOU RESPOND?

It might be impossible to completely escape negativity online. You can't control how others behave. However, you certainly can control how you handle situations.

There are a variety of ways that you can handle this situation. Here's a description of four options.

1. Speak Up.

As soon as the obscene language starts, you can politely tell them that you'd like them to stop. You can tell them that you don't

COMBATTING TOXIC ONLINE COMMUNITIES

Bystanders play a powerful role in combatting online toxicity. Rather than allowing it to continue, they need to "stand up" and speak out against inappropriate behaviors.

appreciate hearing comments like this, especially those directed toward particular groups of people. When they start specifically harassing one of the other gamers, you should immediately stick up for that individual. If there is a specific code of conduct on the site, then you can remind the misbehaving players about these rules. Chances are, your bravery in standng up to these people will spur others to do the same. Start the "mob mentality" in the positive direction and get the rest of the people in the group to use their peer pressure to get the misbehaving gamers to stop.

2. Report them.

If the site has a specific code of conduct and a way to report members with infractions, then use this system. People need to be held accountable for their actions. Unfortunately, for some people it requires punishment from an outside source since their own values and personal code of conduct aren't at a place where they can monitor themselves. Reporting them is really doing them a favor: It will let them know that their behavior will not be tolerated and that they need to clean up their act. This will likely not only help them in their online world but in their real-world life as well.

3. Leave the game.

If you speak up and tell the other gamers to stop and they don't, then your only course of action is simply to leave the game. In real life, if you were in a group and people began behaving a certain way and you didn't like it, you could just walk away. It's actually even easier to do that online than it is in real life! You can just flip the switch on your Xbox, television, or computer and voilà! the toxic situation is immediately gone! It's like magic! You never have to see or deal with those people again. There's a lot of freedom and power in just walking away from a toxic environment.

4. Block Them.

You don't have to continue to play with people like this. Once you report them and leave the game, block these players so you don't have to encounter them again.

REACHING OUT WITH KINDNESS

It is possible to spend time online without encountering negativity. The key to doing so is choosing your online communities wisely. If a website is known to be extremely toxic and you don't want to be impacted by that negativity, then you simply stay off of it! Instead of wasting your time with sites that bring you down, spend your time on sites that are positive and have an uplifting community spirit among their members.

One blog that is particularly impressive for its community-building efforts is *Becoming Minimalist*, a site hosted by Joshua Becker. His article on the website titled "6 Steps to Find More Gratitude in Your Life" is a great example of positive community spirit. The article is fantastic because it helps people improve their lives by increasing their level of gratitude.

Yet, what is most impressive about the piece is actually found in the comments section. Typically, a comments section can be a scary place! When the public forum is open, you never know what you're going to encounter. However, that is not the case with this article. The readers' comments are so wonderful—they share their thanks for his article and give examples of ways his tips have helped their lives. One particular reader mentions his difficulty finding friends and how lonely he feels. A slew of people in this community immediately reached out in support of this individual. They gave suggestions of ways he could feel less lonely and even offered to be his friend. That is the kind of online world that a person wants to be part of: One that lifts others instead of tearing them down.

Scenario #2

You have just read an article online and are curious to see what other people feel about it. You scroll down to the comments section and start to read. Some of the people have very insightful things to say. Yet, there is one troll who is spewing a whole lot of negativity in his (or her) comments. What should you do?

(Note: The troll's comments in this scenario are just negative, benign comments. They aren't filled with threats, harassment, or violence toward an individual or group of people. If that is the kind of troll you encounter, the only recourse is to report the person.)

Trolls are a big problem online. Because of that, there have been numerous articles written that give advice on how to deal with these pests. Here are a few suggestions from the experts:

1. Starve them.

Many experts agree that the best way to silence a troll is to starve them. Trolls want attention and if you just ignore them, they'll have no dialogue to "feed" them. Sometimes this works, and sometimes it doesn't. Sometimes it just irritates the troll and makes the person get louder and harsher in his or her comments.

COMBATTING TOXIC ONLINE COMMUNITIES

Trolls post outlandish things because they want attention. If you give it to them, they will only want more. Try ignoring trolls and see what happens. Most likely, they will wither away when no one feeds them.

2. Don't Argue.

It's pointless to get into an argument with a troll. That's what trolls really want, so in essence you are providing fuel for them and escalating the situation even further.

3. Make Light of the Situation.

Sometimes it's possible to defuse a troll with a joke. Maybe you'll even make the troll, and everyone else, laugh with your wittiness.

Here's a great example of how a supermarket chain in the United Kingdom dealt with a troll on Twitter. A customer tweeted out a message directed at Sainsbury's: "Dear Sainsbury's. The chicken in my sandwich tastes like it was beaten to death by Hulk Hogan. Was it?" Sainsbury's responded with the following tweet: "Really sorry it wasn't up to scratch. We will replace Mr. Hogan with Ultimate Warrior on our production line immediately."

4. Diffuse the Situation with Kindness.

Instead of feeding into the negativity, you could instead send out a positive message directed toward the troll. One example of this happened in November 2015. NFL star Le'Veon Bell received a trollish remark from someone on Twitter after he was injured during a game. The person used several obscenities and said he was glad Le'Veon tore his ACL. Le'Veon responded as follows: "It wasn't my ACL sir . . . but I hope your day brightens up … no1 should b that upset."

5. Report the troll.

Report the troll's comments to the moderators and request that they do something about it. You need to especially do this if the troll is hurling hate speech, violence, or harassment toward a particular individual or group of people.

6. Leave.

You don't have to stay and read the troll's comments. You can always just leave the website and find something more positive to do.

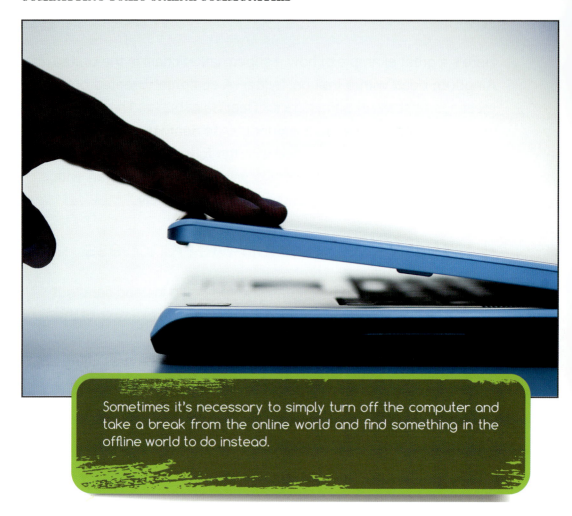

Sometimes it's necessary to simply turn off the computer and take a break from the online world and find something in the offline world to do instead.

Scenario #3

You are on a social media account and a friend posts an unkind remark or an unkind photo about another person who you all know in real life. Many other people have already commented on the photo or comment and have re-shared it. What should you do?

This is a real-life example of mob mentality. You can either be a bystander who does nothing, a bystander who joins the rest of the "mob," or a bystander who actually does something to help the person being cyberbullied. Obviously, the appropriate response to this scenario is the third option. It can sometimes be scary to stand up for what is right, but here are ways that you can do it.

1. Do not reshare.

This is the most obvious way not to get involved in the situation. But this is just one of many things that you should do.

2. Speak Up.

Tell the others that it's not cool what they are doing and you will not participate. Make it clear that you do not think this is funny and you will not be part of this bullying behavior. This is the part that can be very difficult, but if you were the one being bullied, you'd want someone to stand up for you. Peer pressure works. You will be surprised how many other people feel the same way that you do but are too afraid to say something. When you start the ball rolling in a positive direction, many will likely follow along with you. But even if they don't, it's better to be alone and right than with a group and be wrong.

3. Report it.

You should report this behavior to the moderators of the social network and let them deal with the offenders. You can also report it to a trusted adult like a teacher or a school counselor and let them get involved in stopping it.

COMBATTING TOXIC ONLINE COMMUNITIES

If you know someone who has been bullied online or in the real world, reach out and be a friend. You cannot undo what happened to him or her, but showing your support will help a lot.

4. Show support for the victim.

Go visit the person or call him or her on the phone. Let the person know that you are a friend and do not support this type of behavior. The antibullying I Am a Witness (http://www.iwitnessbullying.org) provides some great examples of how to show support for cyberbully victims. Check it out for ideas.

A BRIGHT ONLINE FUTURE

The reality of the matter is that wherever there is good, there is also the potential for bad. The Internet is an amazing place where the world is at your fingertips. You can visit museums from around the world and tour exhibits as if you're standing in the building. You can read books that are found on the shelves of prestigious university libraries. If there's something you want to learn about you can Google it, and in seconds you will have your answers.

However, as this resource has already described, the Internet can also be a very negative place. It can, unfortunately, bring out the worst in human behavior. Teens everywhere have to deal with issues that teens in other generations didn't have to deal with. Cyberbullying and toxic online environments are some of those issues.

According to NoBullying.org, here's how teens were affected in recent years:

- 52 percent of teens said they were cyberbullied this year.
- 55 percent of teens have witnessed others being bullied on social media.
- 95 percent of teens who witnessed bullying on social media just ignored the behavior.
- Less than half of people who were bullied told their parents about the bullying.

Just because these statistics are how things are now doesn't mean that they have to stay that way in the future.

Negative behavior online and cyberbullying do not have to continue. They can be stopped. The most amazing thing about it is that teens really do have the power in their own hands to do something about it and change their world and their online experience into a positive one.

One way that teens can do this is by using examples from the past as examples of what not to do. Think about the Salem Witch Trials and how the people in that era

Cyberbulling is real and many teens are affected by it. But there are many resources available to help those who find themselves on either side of this situation.

went along with the crowd out of fear and suspicion. Don't let that happen to you. If you see someone being "wrongly accused" or treated unfairly online, do something to change that. Don't let yourself get caught up in negative mob mentalities either. Think of what happened to Walter Palmer in the Cecil the lion incident. Don't get so caught up in a "cause" that you forget that a real human being is on the other end of that "cause."

Always be aware of your own behavior. Make sure that you are being accountable for your own actions and behavior online. Remember that the things you do online can stay online forever.

The things you do now as a teen can come back and haunt you later in life when you apply to colleges and jobs. Show your most positive self when you're online and you'll run into less problems later on in life. Frequently refer back to the quiz in chapter two and make adjustments as needed.

Don't go around searching for the negative online. There are so many positive websites out there that you can spend all of your time on the Internet

Be careful what you share online. What may seem like a funny text or photo now could come back to haunt you later on in life. Remember that college admissions committees and future employers may see them.

43

surrounded by positivity and rarely encounter the negative. There's no need to waste your energy or your mind on things that bring yourself or others down.

THE MOST POSITIVE PLACES ON THE INTERNET

In 2013, the *Huffington Post* published an article titled "Inspiring Websites: The 10 Happiest Places on the Internet." Here are some of its suggestions of places to visit for some feel-good energy:

WeStopHate.org. This site is run by teens! It is a nonprofit that is focused on raising the self-esteem of teens. This site gives a place for teens to interact with each other in a positive community environment and watch videos and get helpful coaching from teen experts.

HooplaHa.com The subtitle of this site is "Life with a Smile." It is a collection of positive stories and videos of people from all over the world. Their mission is to "make people smile as much as possible."

Tumblr's Positivity Page: Go to Tumblr and type "positivity" into the search field. Inspiring and uplifting quotes will come tumbling onto your screen.

A BRIGHT ONLINE FUTURE

Surround yourself with a real-life network of support. If you find yourself a victim of cyberbullying or harassment online, don't go through it alone. The first thing you need to do is tell someone about it. You can start with your friends. They may be able to give you some initial support. However, you also need to find trusted adults to talk to as well. They are not inside your teen social world, so they will be able to see things differently than you see them. They will be able to give you advice and help you find solutions. They may not have been through exactly what you are going through, but they were a teen once and they definitely understand what it is like to go through this stage of life. Trusted

Fill your life with positive people and positive things. There's so much good in the world—why waste your time on anything negative and toxic?

45

adults come in all different forms. They can be a family member (parent, aunt or uncle, cousin, grandparent), a religious leader, a scout leader, a guidance counselor, a coach, a teacher, or a neighbor.

There are also many ways to find support online. Organizations such as End to Cyberbullying (http://www.endcyberbullying.org) make it their business to provide people with resources, support, and counseling for instances of cyberbullying. The resources on here are abundantly helpful and give readers the tools they need to handle toxic situations online. The Boys Town organization

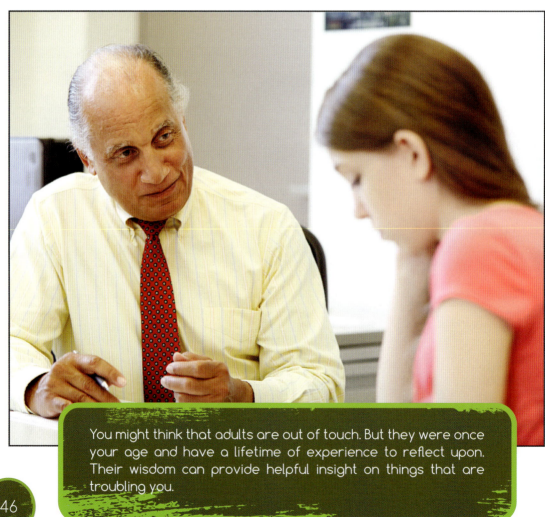

You might think that adults are out of touch. But they were once your age and have a lifetime of experience to reflect upon. Their wisdom can provide helpful insight on things that are troubling you.

(located in Boys Town, Nebraska) is available to help anyone who needs someone to talk to. People can call twenty-four hours, seven days a week, and find a listening ear on the other end of the phone.

TIPS ON HOW TO MAKE THE INTERNET A HAPPIER, MORE POSITIVE PLACE

There are lots of tips on how to deal with negativity in the online world. But how about how to spread positivity?

Here are some ideas:

Post your favorite positive quotes on social media. These can be just in text format or in visual format. For ideas, look here:
- Pinterest: Positive quotes
- Instagram: Positive quotes
- Google: Positive quotes

Post positive comments on the comments sections of websites. Compliment the author and show gratitude for the time he or she took to write the article.

Write uplifting messages to friends in your online communities. Tell them something you think is great

(continued on the next page)

(continued from previous page)

about them or have enjoyed about your interactions.
Be a good sport when you're playing online games.
Share hope-filled videos with others.
Help the lightbulb go on in other's minds by sharing enlightening historical or scientific facts or stories.

If you find that you disagree with someone, either comment back in a positive, respectful way, or just don't comment at all. Everyone is entitled to their own opinion. Value others' opinions like you hope they would value yours.

Internet users do not need to feel powerless online. They can feel empowered by the many wonderful options that they have with this modern piece of technology. It's a place where friendships can be built and fostered, new worlds can be discovered, and lives can be changed for the better. Dr. Suzana Flores, a clinical psychologist and social media expert, was quoted in the *Scholastic Scope* article "Apps of Hate" by Jane Porter in March 2015: "Never before in history have teens had so much power to express themselves so freely to so many people. This is an amazing thing, but with power comes responsibility. You can do so much harm, but you can do so much good too." And how very true that is!

There are ways to combat toxic online environments—the primary way is through personal accountability. The second way is through rules that are made and enforced by the sites themselves. A country cannot exist in a state of anarchy where there are no rules and people are allowed to do anything they

A BRIGHT ONLINE FUTURE

We live in an amazing time, where so many opportunities are available to us. We just need to focus on the good we can bring to our friends, our communities, and to the world!

please. The Internet is a virtual world, so in essence, rules need to be set and enforced in order to keep everyone safe online. Otherwise, anarchy will reign there as well. The combination of both of these methods—personal accountability and rule enforcement—will help decrease the amount of negativity that is found online. The future of the Internet is a bright one—we just need to decide to make it that way!

GLOSSARY

ANONYMITY The state of being anonymous or not acknowledging one's name.

BANDWAGON A large decorated wagon that carries a musical band in a circus parade or political rally.

CYBERBULLYING The act of harassing someone online by sending or posting cruel or mean messages, usually anonymously.

CYBERPSYCHOLOGY The study of human and group behavior in the online world.

DIGITAL FOOTPRINT A "trail" that a person leaves behind on the Internet, which includes his or her activities, actions, and communications.

DISINHIBITION A loss of restraint or inhibition.

FORUM An online meeting place where people can discuss specific topics.

HUMAN PSYCHOLOGY The study of the behavior, actions, interactions, and emotions of human beings

MISOGYNY Dislike, distrust, hatred, or prejudice toward women.

MOB MENTALITY The way people are influenced by their peers to behave a certain way or follow certain trends, just because the group is doing so.

ONLINE CITIZEN A person who participates in any way on the internet.

ONLINE HARASSMENT Using the Internet to threaten, hassle, or stalk another individual.

PERSONAL ACCOUNTABILITY Being responsible for one's own decisions.

GLOSSARY

PURITAN A member of a group of English Protestants who regarded the Church of England as incomplete; many immigrated to New England in the seventeeth century.

SUSPECT A person thought to be guilty of a crime or offense.

TOXICITY The degree to which something is dangerous, poisonous, or harmful.

TROLL A person who deliberately makes offensive, cruel, or provocative online posts.

VIGILANTE JUSTICE Enforcement of the law by individuals or groups that lack the legal authority to do so.

VITRIOL Cruel and bitter criticism.

WITCH HUNT The search for and prosecution of a person suspected of witchcraft.

FOR MORE INFORMATION

Boys Town
14100 Crawford Street
Boys Town, NE 68010
(800) 448-3000
(800) 448-1833 (TDD)
Website: http://www.boystown.org

Boys Town isn't an organization designed to help boys. Rather, it's an organization in Boys Town, Nebraska, that helps teens, parents, and families with free twenty-four-hour-a-day counselors. Translation services in more than 140 languages are also available as well as a TDD line for deaf or hearing impaired callers.

Bullying Canada
471 Smythe Street
PO Box 27009
Fredericton, NB E3B 9M1
Canada
Website: https://www.bullyingcanada.ca

This website is Canada's first youth-created antibullying website. It offers help and support to everyone involved in bullying. The victim, the bully, the bystander, the parents, the school staff, and the community are all offered help through this organization.

CyberAngels Internet Safety Education Program
982 East 89th Street
Brooklyn, NY 11236

FOR MORE INFORMATION

Website: http://www.cyberangels.org
CyberAngels is an online safety education program that teaches children how to use the Internet safely and how to combat bullies and cyberbullies.

Cyber Bullying Prevention
5N426 Meadowview Lane
St Charles, IL 60175
(847) 769-7495
Website: http://www.cyberbullyingprevention.com
Dedicated to raising awareness of cyberbullying and its negative impacts.

Cyberbullying Research Center
5353 Parkside Drive
Jupiter, FL 33458-2906
Website: http://cyberbullying.org
This center is "dedicated to providing up-to-date information about the nature, extent, causes, and consequence of cyberbullying among adolescents." The center is directed by two university professors: one from Florida Atlantic University (Dr. Sameer Hinduja) and one from the University of Wisconsin–Eau Claire (Dr. Justin Patchin).

End to Cyberbullying Organization
147 W 35th Street, Suite 1404
New York, NY 10001
(772) 202-3822
Website: http://www.endcyberbullying.org
The mission of this organization is to raise awareness about cyberbullying and provide resources for those who have

been cyberbullied. It is a state certified nonprofit organization founded in 2011. "ETCB hopes to help teens, parents, educators, and others to identify, prevent, and ultimately stop cyberbullying."

Family Online Safety Institute
400 7th Street NW, Suite 506
Washington, DC 20004
(202) 775-0158
Website: https://www.fosi.org
This organization knows that online safety is everyone's concern. Its mission is to bring a "unique, international perspective to the potential risks and harms as well as the rewards of our online lives."

National Crime Prevention Council
1201 Connecticut Avenue NW, Suite 200
Washington, DC 20036
(202) 466-6272
Website: http://www.ncpc.org
The National Crime Prevention Council aims to be the "nation's leader in helping people keep themselves, their families, and their communities safe from crime." This includes keeping people safe in the real world and online world.

National Suicide Prevention Lifeline
(800) 273-8255
(800) 799-4889 (TTY)
Website: http://www.suicidepreventionlifeline.org
The National Suicide Prevention Lifeline provides twenty-four-hour, seven-day a week counseling to people who feel like

they just need to talk. No matter what problems a person is dealing with, the counselors are prepared to listen, show they care, and help the caller find a positive solution to his/her problems.

No Bully
1012 Torney Avenue
San Francisco, CA 94129
(415) 767-0070
Website: http://www.nobully.org
No Bully is a nonprofit organization. It helps provide training for educational institutions on how to stop bullying and cyberbullying among their student populations. The No Bully System has helped schools across the country create bully-free campuses.

PREVNet
Queen's University
98 Barrie Street
Kingston, ON K7L 3N6
Canada
(613) 533-2632
Website: http://www.prevnet.ca
This organization's goal is to stop bullying in Canada. They are a network of 122 leading Canadian research scientists and 62 national youth-serving organizations. This organization became the first of its kind when it was launched in 2006.

Stop Bullying
Managed by U.S. Department of Health and Human Services
200 Independence Avenue SW

Washington, DC 20201
Website: http://www.stopbullying.gov
This U.S. government website provides information about various types of bullying, including online bullying. This information is collected from various government agencies. It includes details about who is at risk and how online (and real-life) bullying can be prevented.

STOP Cyberbullying
Wired Kids, Inc.
PMB 342
4401-A Connecticut Ave NW
Washington, DC 20008
(201) 463-8663
Website: http://www.stopcyberbullying.org
An organization dedicated to showing children and educators how they can help prevent and take a stand against the practice of cyberbullying.

Websites

Because of the changing nature of Internet links, Rosen Publishing has developed an online list of websites related to the subject of this book. This site is updated regularly. Please use this link to access the list:

http://www.rosenlinks.com/CSTC/toxic

FOR FURTHER READING

Boyd, Danah. *It's Complicated: The Social Lives of Networked Teens.* New Haven, CT: Yale University Press, 2015.

Brown, Tracy. *Cyberbullying: Online Safety* (Helpline: Teen Issues and Answers). New York, NY: Rosen Classroom, 2013.

Brown, Tracy. *Facebook Safety and Privacy* (21st Century Safety and Privacy). New York, NY: Rosen Publishing Group, 2013.

Culp, Jennifer. *Online Gaming Safety and Privacy* (21st Century Safety and Privacy). New York, NY: Rosen Publishing Group, 2013.

Hinduja, Sameer K., and Justin W. Patchin. *Bullying Beyond the Schoolyard: Preventing and Responding to Cyberbullying.* Thousand Oaks, CA: Corwin, 2014.

Hunter, Nick. *Cyber Bullying.* Portsmouth, NH: Heinemann, 2011.

Ivester, Matt. *lol…OMG!: What Every Student Needs to Know About Online Reputation Management, Digital Citizenship and Cyberbullying.* CreateSpace Independent Publishing Platform, 2011.

Merritt, Marian. *Norton's Family Online Safety Guide.* Amazon Digital Services, 2012.

Miles, Lisa. *How to Survive Online Embarrassment* (Girl Talk). New York, NY: Rosen Publishing Group, 2013.

Montgomery, Jim. *Internet Security 2016: Security & Privacy on Laptops, Smartphones & Tablets.* Amazon Digital Services, Inc., 2014.

Orr, Tamra. *Top 10 Tips for Safe and Responsible Digital*

Communication *(Tips for Success)*. New York, NY: Rosen Publishing Group, 2012.

Ryan, Peter. *Online Bullying* (Teen Mental Health). New York, NY: Rosen Publishing Group, 2011.

Weinberger, Jesse. *The Boogeyman Exists, and He's In Your Child's Back Pocket: Internet Safety Tips for Keeping Your Children Safe Online, Smartphone Safety, Social Media Safety, and Gaming Safety.* CreateSpace Independent Publishing Platform, 2014.

BIBLIOGRAPHY

Berry, Eric D. "NFL Star Le'Veon Bell Kills Racist Twitter Troll with Kindness." Hip Hollywood, November 10, 2015. Retrieved December 9, 2015 (http://hiphollywood.com/2015/11/nfl-star-leveon-bell-kills-racist-twitter-troll-with-kindness).

Bittel, Jason. "Why Cecil the Lion Was So Popular with People." *National Geographic*, July 30, 2015. Retrieved December 8, 2015 (http://news.nationalgeographic.com/2015/07/150730-cecil-lion-africa-hunting-science-animals).

Blog.Reddit. "Reflections on the Recent Boston Crisis." April 22, 2013. Retrieved December 8, 2015 (http://www.redditblog.com/2013/04/reflections-on-recent-boston-crisis.html).

Collins, Katie. "Why Outlawing Anonymity Will Not Halt Online Abuse." Wired.co.uk, August 19, 2015. Retrieved December 8, 2015 (http://www.wired.co.uk/news/archive/2015-08/19/real-name-policies-anonymity-online-harassment).

Hankes, Keegan. "The Most Violently Racist Internet Content Isn't Found on Sites Like Stormfront and VNN Any More." Southern Poverty Law Center, March 9, 2015. Retrieved December 8, 2015 (https://www.splcenter.org/fighting-hate/intelligence-report/2015/black-hole).

Hudson, Laura. "Curbing Online Abuse Isn't Impossible. Here's Where We Start." Wired.com, May 15, 2014. Retrieved December 8, 2015 (http://www.wired.com/2014/05/fighting-online-harassment).

Kang, Jay Caspian. "Should Reddit Be Blamed for the Spreading of a Smear?" *New York Times Magazine*, July 25, 2013. Retrieved December 8, 2015 (http://www.nytimes.com/2013/07/28/magazine/should-reddit-be-blamed-for-the-spreading-of-a-smear.html?pagewanted=all&_r=2&).

PhD in Parenting. "Moms, Trolls, Blog Comments and Rebecca Eckler's 'Mommy Mob.'" May 20, 2014. Retrieved December 8, 2015 (http://www.phdinparenting.com/blog/2014/5/20/moms-trolls-blog-comments-and-rebecca-ecklers-mommy-mob.html).

Porter, Jane. "Apps of Hate." *Scholastic Choices*, March 2015, Volume 30, Issue 6, pp. 13–17.

Reddit. "Do Not Threaten, Harass, or Bully." Reddit help. Retrieved December 8, 2015 (https://reddit.zendesk.com/hc/en-us/articles/205701155-Do-not-threaten-harass-or-bully).

Riot Games. "Upgrading the Tribunal." League of Legends. Retrieved December 8, 2015 (http://na.leagueoflegends.com/en/news/game-updates/player-behavior/upgrading-tribunal).

Schley, Lacy. "Mob Mentality Can Take Over Protests or Even Clearance Sales." Medill Reports, May 22, 2012. Retrieved December 8, 2015 (http://newsarchive.medill.northwestern.edu/chicago/news-205860.html).

Slane, Kevin. "Walter Palmer Killed Cecil the Lion. Then the Internet Threatened to Kill Him." BDCwire, July 29, 2015. Retrieved December 8, 2015 (http://www.bdcwire.com/cecil-the-lion).

Steiner, Peter. "On the Internet, Nobody Knows You're a Dog." Condé Nast Collection. Retrieved December 8, 2015 (http://www.condenaststore.com/-sp/On-the-Internet-nobody-knows-you-re-a-dog-New-Yorker-Cartoon-Prints_i8562841_.htm).

Suler, John. "The Online Disinhibition Effect." Retrieved December 8, 2015 (http://users.rider.edu/~suler/psycyber/disinhibit.html).

Wheaton, Wil. "Anonymous Trolls Are Destroying Online Games. Here's How to Stop Them." *Washington Post*, November 11, 2014. Retrieved December 8, 2015 (https://www.washingtonpost.com/posteverything/wp/2014/11/11/anonymous-trolls-are-destroying-online-games-heres-how-to-stop-them).

Zhuo, Julie. "Where Anonymity Breeds Contempt." *New York Times*, November 29, 2010. Retrieved December 8, 2015 (http://www.nytimes.com/2010/11/30/opinion/30zhuo.html).

INDEX

A
accountability, 5, 24–25, 43, 48
anonymity, 18–19, 21, 24
armchair detecting, 14–15

B
Becoming Minimalist, 34–35
behavior, inappropriate
　blocking, 33
　ignoring, 33, 39
　reporting, 33, 39
　speaking out against, 31–32, 39
　supporting victims of, 40
behavior, positive
　sites for, 34–35, 44
　tips for spreading, 47–48
behavior guidelines, 27–29
behavior rating systems, 27
Boston Marathon bombing, 14
Boys Town, 46–47
bullying
　statistics on, 42
　what to do if you are a victim, 39, 40, 45–47

C
Cecil the lion, 15–17, 43
college applications, 43
cyberpsychology, 20–21

D
disinhibition effect, 22

E
Eckler, Rebecca, 23–24
End to Cyberbullying, 46
etiquette, online
　evaluating your own, 25–26, 43
　scenarios, 30–33, 35–40

G
gaming, 21–22, 27–29, 30, 48
Google, 41, 47
gratitude, cultivating, 34

H
handles, 18
harassment
　policies on websites, 27
　what to do if you are a victim, 35, 45–47
HooplaHa.com, 44

I
I Am a Witness, 40
Instagram, 47

J
job applications, 43
"jumping on the bandwagon," origin of phrase, 7–9

L
League of Legends, 28–29

INDEX

M
mob mentality, what it is, 12–13
mommy blogs, 23–24
Mommy Mob, The, 24

O
online communities, what they are, 4

P
Palmer, Walter, 15–17, 43
Pinterest, 47

R
Reddit, 5–6, 14, 27

S
Salem Witch Trials, 9–12, 13, 42
subreddits, 6

T
tribunals, 28–29
Tripathi, Sunil, 14
trolls
    de-escalating situations with, 36
    ignoring, 37
    kindness toward, 37
    reporting, 37
    starving them, 35
    using humor to combat, 36–37
Tumblr positivity page, 44

U
user policies, 6

V
vigilante justice, 15, 16, 17

W
WeStopHate.org, 44
witch hunts, examples of online, 14–17

X
Xbox Network, 27

About the Author

Amie Jane Leavitt graduated from Brigham Young University and is an accomplished author, researcher, and photographer. She has written more than sixty books for children and young adults, has contributed to online and print media, and has worked as a consultant, writer, and editor for numerous educational publishing and assessment companies. To see a listing of Amie's current projects and published works, check out her website at www.amiejaneleavitt.com.

Photo Credits

Cover Ollyy/Shutterstock.com; p. 5 MyImages - Micha/Shutterstock.com; p. 8 John Lund/Blend Images/Getty Images; p. 10 Time Life Pictures/The Life Pictures Collection/Getty Images; p. 12 Eric Feferberg/AFP/Getty Images; p. 16 © Andrew Loveridge/University of Oxford/ZUMA Press; p. 19 Ditty_about_summer/Shutterstock.com; p. 20 Serge Krouglikoff/The Image Bank/Getty Images; p. 22 lipik/Shutterstock.com; p. 23 Tyler Olson/Shutterstock.com; p. 28 PNC/Photodisc/Getty Images; p. 31 Paul Monaghan/Moment/Getty Images; p. 32 omgimages/iStock/Getty Images; p. 36 Calavision/Shutterstock.com; p. 38 Tetra Images/Getty Images; p. 40 © iStockphoto.com/Flamingo Photography; p. 42 © iStockphoto.com/mtreasure; p. 43 Jessica Miller/Photolibrary/Getty Images; p. 45 © iStockphoto.com/franckreporter; p. 46 © iStockphoto.com/monkeybusinessimages; p. 49 © iStockphoto.com/DragonImages; cover and interior pages camouflage pattern Lorelyn Medina/Shutterstock.com; cover and interior pages texture patterns Chantal de Bruijne/Shutterstock.com, foxie/Shutterstock.com.

Designer: Nicole Russo; Editor: Christine Poolos;
Photo Researcher: Carina Finn